DATE DUE

Who Lives on a Towering Mountain?

Rachel Lynette

PowerKiDS press
New York

For my dad

Published in 2011 by The Rosen Publishing Group, Inc.
29 East 21st Street, New York, NY 10010

First Edition

Editor: Joanne Randolph
Book Design: Greg Tucker
Photo Researcher: Jessica Gerweck

Photo Credits: Cover James Gritz/Getty Images; pp. 4, 5, 6, 7, 8, 9, 11, 12–13, 14, 15 Shutterstock. com; p. 10 © www.iStockphoto.com/Jeanne Chaput; p. 16 Tom Brakefield/Getty Images; p. 17 Jack Milchanowski/Getty Images; p. 18 Klaus Nigge/Getty Images; p. 19 Andy Rouse/Getty Images; p. 20 Keith Douglas/Getty Images; p. 21 © www.iStockphoto.com/David Parsons; p. 22 Sylvain Sonnet/ Getty Images.

Library of Congress Cataloging-in-Publication Data

Lynette, Rachel.
  Who lives on a towering mountain? / Rachel Lynette. — 1st ed.
      p. cm. — (Exploring habitats)
  Includes index.
  ISBN 978-1-4488-0680-5 (library binding) — ISBN 978-1-4488-1287-5 (pbk.) — ISBN 978-1-4488-1288-2 (6-pack)
  1. Mountain animals—Juvenile literature. I. Title.
  QL113.L96 2010
  591.75'3—dc22
                                        2010003466

Manufactured in the United States of America

CPSIA Compliance Information: Batch #WS10PK: For Further Information contact Rosen Publishing, New York, New York at 1-800-237-9932

Contents

The Tallest Places on Earth

Have you ever been on a mountain? If you were standing near the top of a mountain, the air would likely feel cold. It might also be very windy. You might see snow and ice, or you might just see bare rocks.

Thousands of people have tried to climb to the top of Mount Everest, but few people reach it. Fewer than 700 people have made it to the top.

With this picture in mind, you might think that not much lives on a mountain. This is not true. Plenty of plants and animals make their homes on mountains around the world.

The tallest mountain in the world is Mount Everest. It is 29,002 feet (8,840 m) tall. Everest is located in the

Himalayas, a **mountain range** in Asia. It is too cold for plants and animals to live near the top of Mount Everest. However, many plants and animals live lower down on the mountain.

The Blue Ridge Mountains, shown here, are part of North America's Appalachian Mountains. They are not as tall as Mount Everest, but they are taller than the nearby land.

Mountains Around the World

There are mountains on every **continent** of the world. The mountains in one part of the world are very different from the mountains in other parts of the world.

Brown bears, such as these, live in forests and mountains in northern North America, Europe, and Asia. Most of the brown bears in the United States live in Alaska.

Mountains in **tropical** areas like South America or Africa have warmer **climates** than mountains on other continents. If you went to Mount Kenya, in Africa, you might see elephants and colobus monkeys in the lower parts of the mountains. These animals could not live in the colder Rocky Mountains, of North America. In the Rockies, animals such as bears and mountain goats have thick coats of fur to keep them warm. Even in warmer climates, the tops of tall mountains can get very cold, though.

The Rocky Mountains are home to countless mountain animals and plants. Its highest peaks can be hard places to live, though, and many have snow on them year-round.

In the Zone

The climate changes as you go up a mountain. Scientists call these different climate areas **zones**. On the lower slopes, the weather is warmer. This is called the montane zone. There may be forests full of many different plants and animals there.

Here you can see wildflowers and grasses growing in an alpine meadow in Glacier National Park, in Montana.

As you climb into the subalpine zone, the weather gets colder. There are still forests in the lower parts of this zone. Bushes, grasses, and wildflowers also do well on this part of the mountain. Many kinds of insects, rodents, and small mammals live among the plants there.

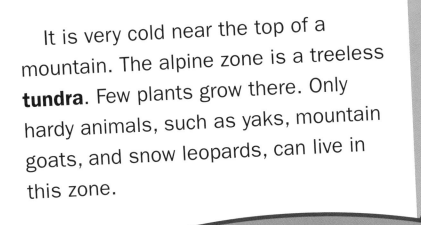

It is very cold near the top of a mountain. The alpine zone is a treeless **tundra**. Few plants grow there. Only hardy animals, such as yaks, mountain goats, and snow leopards, can live in this zone.

Here the treeless alpine zone of the Canadian Rocky Mountains can be seen rising above the tree line.

Living Low on the Mountain

Forests in the lower parts of the mountains are a great **habitat** for many animals. The trees make good homes for woodpeckers, owls, jays, and many other kinds of birds. Squirrels jump from branch to branch.

Mountain lions hunt in the mountains throughout western North America and much of South America. They can be found in many other habitats in those places, too.

Raccoons look for insects and worms among the trees. They also eat fruits, nuts, and small animals. Larger mammals, such as deer, elk, and moose, feed on grass and other plants among the trees. Often these animals look for food higher on the mountain during the summer and **migrate** to the lower

Woodpeckers and other birds make their homes in mountain forests around the world. This woodpecker pecks at a tree to find bugs to eat.

parts during the colder winters. **Predators** such as wolves and mountain lions live in the lower parts of the mountains, too. They move through the forests, looking for animals to eat. These predators often choose animals that are weak or already hurt for their **prey**.

Elks, such as this one, spend their winters in the valleys and lower parts of mountains. In early summer, they move high up into the mountains to have babies.

Black Bears

Black bears can find plenty to eat in the mountain forest because they eat both plants and animals. Animals that eat all kinds of food are called omnivores. During the summer and fall, black bears eat their

Black bears are great at climbing, and cubs often climb trees to stay safe from danger. Cubs, such as this one, stay with their mothers for about two years.

fill of grasses, berries, insects, and small mammals. All that good food gives them extra stores of fat. They need that fat in the winter. They sleep in their dens and do not eat during those cold months.

During the winter, a mother bear may give birth to two or three cubs. Bear cubs stay in the den with their mother until spring. When spring arrives, the mother bear and her cubs come out of the den to look for food.

Meadow Animals

Farther up the mountain, trees give way to meadows and low-lying plants. Which animals live in mountain meadows?

In the summer, butterflies, honeybees, and hummingbirds gather **pollen** and drink the juice from wildflowers.

Marmots hide among the rocks around mountain meadows, whistling when danger is near.

Tiny pikas collect grasses and lay them out on rocks to dry. These rabbit relatives will use the dried grasses for food during the long winter. They also line their burrows with the grasses. Ground squirrels eat as much as they can to get ready for their long winter sleeps.

14

Snowshoe hares have white fur in the winter, as this one does. In the summer, their fur turns brown to blend in with their new surroundings.

During the winter, snowshoe hares hop across the snow-covered meadow. Their white fur blends in with the snow, hiding them from predators. A snowshoe hare has many enemies. A mountain fox, weasel, or hawk may eat one for lunch!

Lots of butterflies come to mountain meadows each summer. A butterfly drinks through its long, strawlike mouth, called a proboscis (pruh-BAH-sis).

Prickly Porcupines

If you were hiking in the mountains, one of the animals you might see is a porcupine. A porcupine's body is covered in sharp, needlelike quills.

A large porcupine can have up to 30,000 quills. The quills break off easily in an enemy's skin, but new quills grow in. Here a mother and baby eat bark from a tree.

A porcupine cannot shoot its quills, but it can make them stand straight out when it is scared. Most predators do not want a mouthful of quills, so they leave the porcupines alone!

Some kinds of porcupines live in burrows or in small caves. Others live in trees. They have curved claws for climbing. Porcupines look for food at night. They eat bark, roots, seeds, flowers, and berries.

Mother porcupines give birth to one to four babies. Baby porcupines are born with soft quills.

A baby porcupine's quills get harder during the first few days of life. This young porcupine's quills are not soft anymore.

On Top of the World

Animals that live near the top of a mountain must **adapt** to the harsh climate. Yaks, alpacas, and mountain goats have thick coats of fur to keep them warm. Snow leopards have thick coats, too.

This is an American bald eagle. Bald eagles like to eat fish best. They may make their homes on coasts or by large lakes and ponds in mountains or other forested places.

They also have long bushy tails that they curl around themselves when they sleep. Most of these animals are great climbers, too. This is useful when they make their way up steep, rocky mountainsides.

Many birds, such as eagles, hawks, and falcons, look for food on the mountaintops. It is easy for them to spot their prey near the top of the mountain because there are no trees to provide protection to small animals.

Snow leopards live high up in the mountains of Central Asia. They like to live on steep, rocky cliffs best. These big hunters can jump up to six times their body length.

Bighorn Sheep

Bighorn sheep can be found high up in the mountains of North America. These sheep are known for their large, curved horns. The horns of a male bighorn sheep can weigh up to 30 pounds (14 kg).

Here two bighorn sheep fight by hitting their horns together. The bones are extra thick behind their horns to keep the sheep from hurting their heads.

That is as much as all the other bones in his body weigh together! Male bighorn sheep use their horns to fight each other. They charge at each other at speeds of 20 miles per hour (32 km/h). The winner of the fight gets to lead the herd.

Bighorn sheep have split hooves that are perfect for climbing rocky slopes. They can climb to tufts of grass that other animals cannot reach. They can also escape predators by climbing high on the mountain.

A group of female bighorn sheep stand on a cliff in Colorado. Female bighorn sheep's horns do not get as big as the males' horns do.

Living in the Mountains

It is not easy to live in the mountains. Mountain animals must be able to keep their bodies warm. They must be able to climb the steep mountain slopes. Animals that do not **hibernate** must find enough food to live through the winters.

Mountains can be beautiful places to walk with your family. Just be careful to leave nature as you found it.

If you go to the mountains, treat the plants and animals you find there with respect. Stay on the trails so you do not step on the plants. Make sure not to leave litter behind. Mountain animals need habitats that are not overrun with people and pollution.

Glossary

adapt (uh-DAPT) To change to fit new conditions.

climates (KLY-mits) The kinds of weather certain places have.

continent (KON-tuh-nent) One of Earth's seven large landmasses.

habitat (HA-buh-tat) The place where plants and animals naturally live.

hibernate (HY-bur-nayt) To spend the winter in a sleeplike state.

migrate (MY-grayt) To move from one place to another.

mountain range (MOWN-tun RAYNJ) A series of mountains.

pollen (PAH-lin) A yellow dust made by the male parts of flowers.

predators (PREH-duh-terz) Animals that kill other animals for food.

prey (PRAY) An animal that is hunted by another animal for food.

tropical (TRAH-puh-kul) Having to do with the warm parts of Earth that are near the equator.

tundra (TUN-druh) The icy, treeless land of the coldest parts of the world, including some mountaintops.

zones (ZOHNZ) Large areas.

Index

A
animals, 4–12, 14, 16,
    18–19, 21–22

C
climate(s), 6–8, 18

E
Everest, Mount, 4–5

F
food, 10, 12–14, 17,
    19, 22
forest(s), 8, 10–12

H
Himalayas, 5

homes, 4, 10

I
ice, 4

K
Kenya, Mount, 6

M
monkeys, 6
mountain range, 5

P
part(s), 6, 8, 10–11
plants, 4–5, 8–10, 12,
    14, 22
pollen, 14

predators, 11, 15–16, 21
prey, 11, 19

R
Rocky Mountains, 7

S
snow, 4, 15
South America, 6
summer, 10, 12, 14

T
top(s), 4–5, 7, 9, 18–19
tundra, 9

Z
zone(s), 8–9

Web Sites

Due to the changing nature of Internet links, PowerKids Press has developed an online list of Web sites related to the subject of this book. This site is updated regularly. Please use this link to access the list:
www.powerkidslinks.com/explore/tm/